Disfortune

Disfortune

POEMS BY

Joe Wenderoth

Wesleyan University Press

Published by University Press of New England

Hanover and London

Wesleyan University Press

Published by

University Press of New England,

Hanover, NH 03755

© 1995 by Joe Wenderoth

All rights reserved

Printed in the United States of America

5 4 3 2 1

CIP data appear at the end of the book

The publisher gratefully acknowledges
the support of Lannon Foundation in
the publication of this book.

If poetic speech could be
for a specific other,
this book would be
for Sandy Brown.

Thank you firstly and above all to my teacher and worldly (this- and other-) protector, Heather McHugh. Any intelligence in this book might be hers. Thanks also to Alan, Michael, Michael, Karen, Steve, Laura, Stuart, and Arty. Thanks to my dad for the endless xeroxing. Thanks to Dwight Yoakam for his kind permissions. Thanks to the people at NYU who helped me, and special thanks to the remarkable community of writers at Warren Wilson College.

"For it would be better for us not to be

rather than always be ours."

— BERNARD OF CLAIRVAUX

Contents

I.

II.

III.

I.

Yellow-Jacket Devouring Live Cicada

in the weeds and wildflowers
just off the path
I notice the patience
of this yellow-jacket
and the quiet (not audible
from afar) as it tears loose
the strings of its instrument
as it removes sound
from the song
which brightens
as it comes
less and less often
though still nourishing
the killing body
with a rhythm too ordinary
and too beautiful
to stand
playing

Man, woman.
There is a brevity
that does not fade,
does not fail
to leave painful.
For us,
for anyone.
Bathe in the spark
of this or that doomed business.
Be silent with me
in the house; sleep
in front of me.
Just before, though,
tell me how cold the day
on the other side
of our dream, dreamt
or not, will be.

Extravagance Of Any Body

My body is a holiday season
in which the blessed day arrives too soon,
losing years in hours, the one
no longer or brighter
than the other, or the next.

My body is not grateful,
not precise, having suddenly so much
to prepare for, so much to keep
from saying. And yet,
even so, even hard-pressed,
it asks nothing of me.

My body acts as though I'm not even here,
as though I've never spoken.
It is, in this, unthinkably kind.
Its extravagant kindness is painful
to behold; it has given me *time*.
A glass of water, for example,
is the idea of an hour.

We find it very very easy to be true.
For instance: This morning has to do with animals.
Can't see 'em, they're implied.
Animals, just beyond each and every horizon.
Not ANY WAY WE LIKE.
Not ANY WAY THEY LIKE.
But definite, definite as our very pretty
living room, which is just
our not having sentences.
Definite animals, not here.
Only here in sentences going unspoken.
    "Good morning animals."
    "It's not a good morning," the animals say.
    "Please go away."

That's when the talking-singing, the whole talking-
singing ball of yarn, begins to unravel.
We start to dread the fact
that a little quiet is all it can really ask.
It gets quiet, and none of us mean it.
When none of us mean it, it's not a good morning.
The animals are right.
We've never seen them.
    "Maybe we should look around for you a bit."
    "Maybe you should put your eyes out," the animals say.
Maybe!
When the animals say maybe, our worries disappear.
We have to feel a little festive even.
All our holidays, since the beginning of the talking-singing,
have sprung up from the empty threats of the animals,
the animal maybe.
It's simply *wonderful* when the animals say maybe.

Pencil a sacred day on to the calendar, friends—
the animals are unsure of themselves!
Our best day is again upon us.
Let us loudly exchange precious gifts.

If you look closely,
knowingly, a character in your own dream,
you can see where we welded his gold arm
to his tin shoulder, and where brass elephants
are obediently interlocking trunks
to solder the bond, tight as your fist.
If you look closely,
the quiet of his hollow body holds you
even tighter, as though a cat
was firmly clenching your forefinger
in its mouth. You draw blood
each time you pull away.
The pain, even the blood, is real,
and you can taste it the moment you wake,
where, in the background, someone is almost
shouting, "you're kidding, you are, you're kidding."

Alone Throwing Stones

FOR DAVID THANNER

When I was ten I walked seriously
down steep steps to a dead river where schools
of minnows rocked in the shallows three or four
feet out. At low tide there was a small beach
of smooth stones and dead fish—catfish, sunnies,
yellow perch. Sometimes, walking the beach
to the point, where the river released itself
into the oblivion of the bay, I was stunned
by the comfort of death, the pure resignation,
a big stinking turtle in dry sand,
or a prize rockfish with eyes rotted out.
These finds, though, were rare as death
in the family, and I lost interest in them
within the hour, each fast becoming
a funeral for someone whose voice
it seemed I had heard just one time,
and who never had reason to speak to me.
The hours I've kept, and keep,
even as I speak, I spent alone throwing stones
as hard as I could
into the dense swaying constellations
of small fish forever plainly before me
in the water, and watching them scatter,
sometimes untouched away, sometimes one or a few
split in half, or just grazed, spinning silver
and frantic to the surface, a sudden
absence of the river's intelligence in them
that satisfied me, each school quickly re-
forming under the dirty little waves.

9

there are more skillful arsonists
hidden in the city gates
than ever before

burned down roads
burned down insects
burned down tools
burned down tigers
everything reduced
a faint stink now
beneath lovely moving pictures
in a million soft rooms

sad Republic
America is still
just weak night genesis
a dream of definite oceans
and polite soldiers

listen to the careful voices
perfectly useless
because of what in you
the flame cannot touch

Learned From Billie Holiday

Pleasure comes easy as pain
is familiar. I've lost interest again
in escape stories, the vague path
of narrative, its tireless
original artists.
It's May in Baltimore City,
late afternoon,
the same nameless lovers
in a bed beside huge windows.
Someone is selling white flowers.
The moon is visible.
I had forgotten about the moon, flowers.
I'm not above it either, the moon and flowers.

Aesthetics Of The Bases Loaded Walk

Four times the pitch is outside the strike zone:
high, low, outside, low—four balls.
The man must be given a base, a base on balls.
But there is no base to be given,
no base unoccupied, the bases are full.
Some cannot understand this.
They believe it must be a shameful thing,
lowly forfeit,
the humiliation of man-made rules and chalk boundaries.
They imagine confrontation itself has failed.
Some, even most, don't understand the bases loaded walk,
and they proceed to hiss
or to mock their earlier earnest applause.
But I love it.
They've got no room to put him on.
They put him on. They put him on
and here comes the lowly run
home. Certain, uncontested,
and incomparably calm.
A home-run would have been unbelievable—
the grand slam, loveliest of moments
to glimpse—
but it leads quickly, inevitably, away from us.
Bases empty.
Rally as good as over.
But a walk! a walk! Bases still loaded!
Rally never at a more urgent or capable point!
This is the beauty of it.
The maintenance of a simple danger by way of a good eye.
The inning, the game itself,
hangs in the indelicate balance

of this subtlest method for staying alive,
in the casual implication of unending loss,
in the terrible patience of an anonymous victory.

Daily News, March Into April 1993

BURNED ALIVE STABBED
RUN DOWN
SHOT IN HEAD

STOLEN

BEATEN DOWN RUBBED OUT
STRANGLED
BRAINWASHED ABANDONED
BLINDED
BLOWN TO BITS

given time
given time

Spring Has Again Needlessly

O the grass is neither silent nor sweet.
Spring has again needlessly
washed my whole walk
and broken nothing.
It has broken nothing, in fact,
too many times
to be spoken to.
That is, to be trusted.

Bus-Ride North To Baltimore

One feels like a hero,
driven from where there isn't safety
toward where there will not be safety.
Which is to say, sleeping in pain,
then with pain.
I freely admit my being
a hero.
A hero then an idiot,
a hero then an idiot.
The idiot hopes to die at the right time,
the hero at the wrong.

In The Sentence Of Sleep

In the sentence of sleep we are the object,
never the subject—I mean we do not sleep,
but are forever slept . . .
by something unclear, something unjust,
something like the first moment of music.
The very first little tune, first played up.
In the sentence of sleep,
we are the curious absence
of those first unforgettable notes.
We say, There are obviously secret plans
to make our way back to the first verse
and to sing it together.
We say, O yes there are clearly big plans
to sing the want all over—something like:
We want the sun as much as it wants us.
This is what we say that we will sing.
In the sentence of sleep,
our singing is an unnamed disease,
unfeared, hereditary,
its harmless low-grade fever
breaking earlier every day.
In the sentence of sleep
we've never wanted anything
but to get well, and we—
each one of us, alone—
can reasonably expect a complete recovery.

Things Written During Dwight Yoakam's Voice

far too at ease I am
far too certain about who
is speaking
when the poem is going on—
how can I convince you of this
this fact:
I wake up crying

Sick, sick, down.
Never naked, waking up
someplace. The sun,
naturally, in my face.
The cause, really.
If there was a way

The only time I feel the pain
The only conquered evening, darlinged away.
A color so barely varied
it's barely worth mentioning.
A color lost, for my sake,
for the sake of the dream
being a dream. And where
it is. *Is*
in the sunshine and the rain

Passage: *Away From The Handlessness Of The Light*

since I've been sick
I build my dream-boat
at all times

the more I don't come
out of the rising
hull-dark
into the handlessness of the light

the more the actual
embarking day
shrinks back into the distances
of its one good story

the more the one good dark
of that one good story
lies me down

the more the girlish shape
of the dream itself
is beside me

and founders
abandoned in the dry

I hammer the womb lightly.
I rush the good things.
I wait patiently in dull songs, well sung.
I clean lit lights.
I eat the roots, the stems, the petals,
in increasingly relative silence.
I help hide the idea of walking.
I go at evening like a primary number
as far down into heaven as I can,
dead wrong.
I keep my hands in my hands,
and my mother's hands in what must not be.
I forget about my lovers.
I remain standing, a dying alarm
in broad crowded daylight,
coming back to myself in less
and less possible waves.

They don't,
simply by saying that something has been lost.

Phone-Call With My Mother

The womb is not deaf—in fact,
the womb hears the heart better,
hears before the deafness of the hands,
and before the too-loud ugly deaf talk
the hands make, even sing in.
The hands themselves are an idea
among many ideas that the womb has.
So this isn't craft, Mom,
what I'm always telling you,
long-distance, always.
This is death-bed whisper
grown young,
and we're still going,
we're going.
I mean we're not staying.
Forgiven? I don't know
even who it is we're leaving,
all this time.

O but all rooms are the same,
promising significant extinctions.
I don't intend to build, Mom.
I don't want anything but what's given—
it's enough,
day, night,
a sentence now and then.
No, that's where you're wrong—
not all days are the same,
though they promise nothing,
each to each.
Listen, here we are again
in that one long summer's

woods, entering the deep shade
of a riverless boatyard.
So dim, the bright green leaves,
old boats. Old paint, faded,
peeling away. The day is dark.
Time to get to work.

What You Don't Want To Happen Won't Happen

Our prayers are not ours,
as a dying fire
isn't its own.

Each star drifts closer,
making money talk.

In the bright, whatever carries
our prayers away from us
swallows its own horses.
The horses swallow whatever pulls them.
It's all downhill.
We must move faster, further.
Now begins the long long wedding.
What kind of vehicle is it
that goes only downhill?

Autobiography Of A Born Singer

Early, I was a wind which swayed
a field of light into
and out of itself, which was mine
none of the time, though I kept it.
I was, that is, for the good of the field
of light, which swayed, as I said.

Late, I was the good sense the blood
used to find its way into
where it's from, past and future
being strictly that speakable place of blood
I will never arrive at.

At all times I stood in the dark,
unstemming the blood, listening
to the vague, lazy begging of what isn't,
to be, what is, to sleep.
But I was opposed to vague,
and my opposition made the begging sound
like it was just a song; I sought to sing along.

Since, my poor voice has revealed the field
of light for what it is, a field of no faces,
and for what it isn't, swaying,
this evening, keeping me.

The Senate

What they heard
was only the singing
that allowed the ship.
What they did not hear—
what they have never heard—
is the design of the hull,
which is, among friends at work,
always spoken,
never sung or written down.

II.

Detailed History Of The Western World

where the river gets swift
my grandfather stops rowing
turns round
and with one oar
sweeps a row-boat full of cats
into water so black
you could say
it was almost anything

Like Blood From A Deep Cut

Like soap-opera deaths, these days are not
believable, but make a week, a summer,
a few years, caught in the only plot,
quickly, muted now, repeating.
Every rough stone is smoothed, every push
of this warm river slower, colder.
This has become obvious.
What is not obvious is daytime itself
appearing in a pointed silence
like a dead relative in a good dream.
The closer that face comes
the quicker the day goes,
the louder the silence asks you to stay.
To say.
Something tells me this is my afternoon.
Something tells me this is my afternoon,
and it comes to me, like blood
from a deep cut, escaping steadily,
no matter what pressure is applied.

All The Hurry

I am the marrying
kind.
Though these muscles will not
us make.
The carriage will stay
empty,
empty and surer.
I am fast, I'm sorry.
Dreams don't start.
Love won't end.

what you said
stops its animals
too often
for the real issue
to be fit

to be tied

"The Most Beautiful World Is Like A Heap Of Rubble, Thrown Down In Confusion"

—Heraclitus, fragment 124

FOR MAGGIE

corner of 9th and 15th drunk
and leaving the loud hour
barely standing and casually turning
to stone
and gnashing of eyes
        you and I
drift by a man
who's wearing a skirt
        and is
all made-up
standing on the curb
waiting for cars
sweet-bitter gnashing of eyes
 to ease
to drift hurting themselves
by

as we are
next to him
he pulls up the skirt
and nothing's under but his un-
usually big dick he handles
so easily

pulls some blood into
strokes it down and lets it hang
thick and white
with his balls

in the humid summer street
in plain
view

and I can't stop looking back
as we pass
looking ahead as we return
always
return forever
from and unto this big brief
absence of stone
and gnashing and drifting
of eyes
    you and I
caught this night
in an exacting
love
a love that keeps
unkeeping us
where we could have it
and have none of it

Demerol

sewn into the lymph-
couch, your sembling
residue

softly catches
everything

on fire;
by this
here panted light
you compose
the necessary *tired*
and then do not play it
do not sing
but only listen—
with your hand

no one stops
the sore fabric of sleep
getting knit getting knit
getting knit

Calling Through Bushels Of Dead Crabs: Dream

come grayly
if need be
grave-bushel in dreams

let all my own
dead therein
seem to move
because the one still
alive at the bottom
knows my hand is there
in the above
in my understanding
meat

only let the dead
I need to reach
through seem
to move

The Voices Of Older Girls Standing Together
In The Calm Dirty Ocean

pre-wild Mom-fires
keep the crowded
Aviation Museum

comfortable

one obsolete cock-pit
leads to
an other

morning mines
this deep,
    outcome
of plated light,

night's white
    closed
into spoken drift,
the always of which
feeds

my several sleep-shades,

which are nothing
but night's white,
a few minutes
nearer
the most minor operation:
there is

Outside The Hospital

He says
when they made this place
they sure knew what they were doing.
He carries the dead woman
everyday from her grave
in the shining sky down
into a small garden,
where a light snow is falling.
He is her lover,
and he brings her here,
knowing he is not allowed to bring her here.
She sees the flowers he's planted
and thanks him
and tells him what their names are.
He says he will never forget them.
The two lie on the ground
beside snow-dusted flowers.
She's in love with the ground
and the flowers,
but not with their names,
and not with him, who is saying them.
She hears him, feels his face
next to her face.
Disappearing forever is the only solution.

Poem: An Illocal Custom
Which Must Be Half-Forgotten

nowhere special I can't
hear you
I'm just a the
upon
your shore

river of children you are
never loud enough
to go unlistened
to

Death

the indifference
of rain
for where

it falls
not going
unnoticed

Feeding A Talking Bird

(there were only regional seductions
before I said)
now that I am, I am,
and you are

mending surgery curtains

(the numerous surgeries have been
taught to speak, and I am

only these, only these)

and you are mending, only mending
surgery curtains,

keeping what they keep

quiet, in a little
while

Time is fine, finally.
The shades you're
        piled living
in
    turn
as they must,
as whatever
sleepers
        the light
asks for.
The pain, the pain
is just,
is just
that
    the light:

Heart-stopping, with, with.
Come to me.
With
the sea.

Come back soon,
like never,
before.

You there, like before never.
At heart, stopped sea.
At sea, a sea.

Prayer

fix me, a blast

A Talking Bird Refuses To Title His Poems

heart-bells in the halting ground
ring, keeping
the come
of we-trees
from spills, and loss
of tune

—dear Jesus
now daylight
will have to be
equally clapperless

*

Some days are gone
before one has appeared
to oneself
in them. The ground,
then, is made of voices,
and You are not my brother,
and You are not my sister.

*

Somehow to leap from the lowest dream
of agility like always
into the pupil-black river
of day—the pure once
of your own voice.
Just to sing the song that's kept you
quiet
all this time.

You

in a dream I was as much alone
as dreams require
though you sat beside me
in an ugly little theater
a dull movie playing—
if I looked up
it's all I could see
I barely looked up
I was listening to you
as you watched
I had nothing of my own
I had this dream

The Flat Road Runs Along
Beside The Frozen River

The man dying in the bed
thinks of riding a bicycle,
slow, standing up.
It is winter and the flat road
runs along beside a frozen river.
Always something has happened
before his riding away.
He can't say what, then or ever.
There is a woman by the side of the bed.
She is the one he is riding away from
in his thought.
He is riding toward where he is.
The woman places an empty bowl
on his chest and looks at him.
He closes his eyes, but still,
he knows she's there.
The bowl is full of blood,
and his heart cannot lift it, even once.
He is standing up on the bicycle.
"The bowl couldn't be full of blood,"
he says, looking down the bright flat road,
and the dying must start all over again.

III.

Early Winter Afternoons

If you stay in a dark room long enough
outside it is nearly as dark; you'll get
to see well enough, and you'll be able
to get around in your mind, like
an old woman in her dreams, turned
steadily into sleep, her fingers
gnarled branches, snakes clasping
an old wooden cane, stronger than both her legs.
You can ask yourself, "what happened?"
but you don't even know where she is now,
or who she was when her face was bright
to see your face.
It was as if she loved you, you recall,
staring at your own same hands in the dark.
She was not light, for them, but only
someone who could not know what they wanted,
someone absent, whom you touched this darkness
with.

Unplumbable

"There is at least one spot in every
dream at which it is unplumbable—a
navel, as it were, that is its point of
contact with the unknown."
—*S. Freud*

The night land sleeps.
It conceals and heals

in one easy step.
It lets something sub-

stantial slip.
It has one dream,

which is not ever
remembered, though

it is spoken of
at all times.

Phonograph

Startled awake to piss, only
in the deepest part of the night
do I sometimes hear
the faint exact music
that I am. Strange
thin face, small hands,
moon-bright cock, more itself
than ever, the faint exact
music that I am.
I take myself in hand.
So heavy, such an old album,
flawless black
in the yellowing sleeve—
and almost obsolete now,
grooves worn away,
the tired chorus skipping,
never ending, true, but sinking away
into the deafening surge
of increasingly mechanical tides,
merciless as the room I sleep in,
this side of the diamond.

For An Inspecific Sorrow

Left alone, I may paint a beautiful picture
or something.
Even late fall winds can't budge
the afternoon light.
I suggest beating yourself with a stick
if the mind is boundless
and still.

To My Fathers

with the horny pump
hid good
in the grown shadows
of the likely story

even the oldest stem of bone
(even the thickest real blood petal
in the whole walk)
is food for the opinioning
mouth
of a crowded wind

—and I see your catchy songs
one after the other
bending to bless the dust-pile
of poor voices in good standing

passing a grill under a bright umbrella
at each corner
mid-town
the smell of meats cooking
in a gentle steady rain

not much music
in these parts
not much pain-fashion

but every now another face
given up to the god
of arbitrary currents
and I am
crossing 18th or 19th Street
walking up Fifth Avenue
without an umbrella myself
gentle rain getting old and heavy
and the implications at an all-time low

Disfortune

the year I was sick
and you took care of me
the most beautiful thing I saw
I saw   lying in the gutter
near a small public basketball court
I played on   alone on weekdays
in a neighborhood where working people lived
it was a blurry polaroid
of two children at a birthday party
one looking at the other
the birthday boy
lustfully

it was over-exposed   scratched up and torn
and had some kind of oil on it
but I took it home
and pinned it up on a cork bulletin board
in the hall outside my rented bedroom
in east Baltimore

then I moved   and left it there
to the unoriginal
oblivion   that made it
and never really ever
let it alone

Pain-Song

Mostly I just sit alone with my radio.
I reckon, in possession
of where,

song-pain.
Wherever else there is

is wanted,
is not,
is not wanted.

Lose Hold Of The Blessing

I love the body in the night,
the body asleep, the body kept
by long dreams. The Fugitive,
The Honeymooners, Bewitched.
Dragnet, Emergency.
Happy Days, Get Smart,
Fantasy Island, Gunsmoke.
Lose hold of a body, even
a split-second, like in a sneeze,
and doors everywhere bang open wide,
and there are new young men
in the dark yard.

Thanksgiving

I was thinking about something all day

I was in a warm house
eating meat
and it was snowing

in no time
it had gotten dark
and I was thinking
about something
all day
when I looked up at the night sky
still full of white clouds

Leaving A Moving Picture Matinee

Beautiful to walk out of the theater
into wide day. The faint bright voices
I don't hear anymore, but remember.
Things
returning lazily but surely
to work, placing this moment
like a cold white egg in my hands.
Things.
Knowing the afternoons's voices
were a pin and a straw,
that what they say
is by now
completely hollowed out.
Knowing the contrived delicacy
of what is emptied and kept, painted
in red, yellow, green, and sky-blue.
Knowing the entire surface is covered
with voices, ancient patterns
at one time meant to remember the dead—
evolved to pure shape now,
no longer recalling anyone.
Knowing that not a speck of white shows.
Things, things knowing,
and in knowing, placing
this moment, a heavy white
egg, in my hands.

Wallace Stevens Describing The Need For And Then The Consequences Of Elvis Presley

Asleep establishments
grounded rumours
of the most alarming kind,
involving your honorable house
in the value of enjoying   (dominion
its own executive defacto,   is really
according to the practice   at an end)
of former instances.

*

Surprise children,
delivered from the insolence
of usefulness,
did not make the afterwards.
Doubtless a rude machine,
sweet-hearts
looked only to the probable
immediate, employed still
by deaf seeming.
As the song became more
endless, its finer weft
nevertheless rose
and wrecked the town.

Wallace Stevens Lecturing
At The Community College

When Americans say *realist* they mean *materialist*.
And yet, we find that there is no such thing
as matter—at least not in the sense
of an essentially abiding, essentially owned
or secured particularity of circumstance.
Which is the sense, by Americans, intended.
When Americans say *realist*
they draw attention to the fact that *the real*
is precisely what they are oblivious to;
at the same time, they devalue the process—
imagination—in which their identities are invested.
They are, in this casual mean usage of the word
real, thoroughly imaginary beings
who altogether distrust, or *know better than*,
the imagination . . .
These people are odd: anti-here *and* anti-there.
I'm afraid, that is, that they have really,
if not truly, gone to heaven.
Many have gone as far as to say so.
They are as powerfully unimportant as heaven,
that much is clear—or they would be,
if they didn't tend to have the money.
Which, I think,
after all, is all
they mean.

"Flowers Are A Tiresome Pastime"

—W. C. Williams

with Williams it's always this certain
flower in a certain light at a certain
time of year on a particular piece
of furniture, always the certainty
is different than it ever was before,
told by a color, keeping us all
where we are—though I have had no way
to know where this is, exactly, not living
myself in the midst of flowers, flowers'
names, I have understood
the one worsening season of color
only vaguely, moving quickly on
to the introduction of the unspeaking
hero, the degree of day,
the non-flower objects, broken of course
and appearing where they will,
where I do get his drift, mine

but today I found myself understanding
Williams' flowers, none of them
in front of me, none in names, I was
riding the subway over to Astor Place
to get my hair cut for cheap, and I began
to see in my car the beautiful faces
of the ugly, rising and staying, blooming
a moment somewhere beneath my voice,
then leaving, not,
obviously, in petals,
but going completely dark,
feeding the necessary never, returning,
given to the bottom of the light

for scattering, and these are his damned
flowers, and for once I wasn't allowed
to turn toward the necessary never
and to hear it speak, hear it pronounce
the dark world's further dim my own,

but took instead the mute bloom of faces
up like breath, like a breath
was what was mine, I took to saying
while it held itself *that* it held itself,
as I have been held, every minute of my life,
by no one I know.

Someone Who Purely Looks The Part

AFTER MARTIN STEPHENSON

A dead rabbit
in the cool sunny street
of the near-empty mobile-home park.
This morning, head pulled away
at the broken neck,
attached to the body
by just a flap of fur.
The open throat is black
in the sun, and darkest
red; wasps and flies gather
thriving into its need
to come apart and become the ground.
I'm on the way to work.
There is time, there,
to kiss a statue.

Knowing then like anyone
only what I know, an unworn body,
the necessity of going on without
myself, going on. I'm almost
alone, save this breath
against the back of your neck,
this arm under your breasts, save
this heart's beat.
Eyes closed, I'm trying to imagine
the shape of your face,
and there is at last time
for such shapes, there is *at last*,
kept by the weak pulse of others' voices,
erratic as a weak pulse can be, the sound
of someone I'll never speak to
lazily hammering in the room above us,
you and I, sleep and waking, led into
and out of ourselves
by useful violence, precise, now,
now again, the unspoken wholly acceptable
sleep of musics, dying out, dying into
our dullness and wanting nothing more
than to get old there, if that is possible,
to be old
when the moment of our faces
is finally allowed.
Old music is the idea of this place,
into which they are leading us away,
these angels, ancestors,
whoever the musicians, in fact,
turn out to be.

Probably A Strong Undertow

I have never seen the way
        they have to stand.
Never seen the shapes
        of the instruments.
Never suspected their useless colors
        kept any secrets.
This water—this is what we say,
        "water—"
this water is dim.
The musicians, like myself, are under
        dim.
They see less than I do,
        and seem less.
And the music comes apart and stays,
comes apart
and stays.
No one knows why it began
        to bother them, or why
they began to draw a crowd,
wading out.

Notes and Acknowledgments

"Morning Fiction." The first line is something like a line in a song that Johnny Cash sings.

"Things Written During Dwight Yoakam's Voice." The lines in italics are lyrics from three different songs on Dwight Yoakam's album *If There Was a Way*, and appear by permission as follows: "IF THERE WAS A WAY" (Dwight Yoakam). © 1990 COAL DUST WEST MUSIC. All rights administered by WARNER-TAMERLANE PUBLISHING CORP. All Rights Reserved. Used By Permission. "IT ONLY HURTS WHEN I CRY" (Dwight Yoakam, Roger Miller) (50% share). © 1990 COAL DUST WEST MUSIC and ADAM TAYLOR MUSIC. All rights on behalf of COAL DUST WEST MUSIC administered by WARNER-TAMERLANE PUBLISHING CORP. All Rights Reserved. Used By Permission. "NOTHING'S CHANGED HERE" (Dwight Yoakam, Kostas) (50% share). © 1990 COAL DUST WEST MUSIC and SONGS OF POLYGRAM INTERNATIONAL INC. All rights on behalf of COAL DUST WEST MUSIC administered by WARNER-TAMERLANE PUBLISHING CORP. All Rights Reserved. Used By Permission.

"The Senate." Before modern times, the design of a ship's hull was closely guarded; often, it was never written down, for fear it would be stolen.

"Autobiography Of A Born Singer." This poem arose to some degree out of my reading about research being done on the difference between the right and left brain. In particular, it alludes to the fact that the familiarity of faces is almost always processed on the side of the brain *not* possessed of language ability.

"Calling Through Bushels Of Dead Crabs: Dream." I've worked steaming and sorting Maryland blue crabs. Sometimes bushels sat in refrigeration for a week or more; when one eventually sorted through these bushels (to separate the crabs by size and quality) they were almost entirely dead. A bushel tends to die, for various reasons, from the top down, such that the crabs that were still alive were usually closer to the bottom. As one reaches into the bushel-basket to discard the dead, the few surviving sense a hand descending, and they *move*, causing the dead on top of them to move, and to seem alive. This is confusing to the sorter, and this ghostly confusion is partly the origin of this poem. The other locatable part of its origin is the phenomenon of dreaming about long hours of reaching into a basket of sharp-bodied, biting creatures . . . after having spent long hours reaching into a basket of sharp-bodied, biting creatures.

"Leaving A Moving Picture Matinee." The pin and the straw and the egg-painting in this poem allude to the process of creating Ukrainian Easter eggs.

Some of the poems in this book have been published previously: *American Poetry Review*, "False Idols"; *Black Warrior Review*, "Alone Throwing Stones"; *Prairie Schooner*, "The Senate," "Like Blood From A Deep Cut"; *TriQuarterly*, "Aesthetics Of The Bases Loaded Walk," "The Flat Road Runs Along Beside The Frozen River," "Flowers Are A Tiresome Pastime"; *Connecticut Poetry Review*, "All The Hurry."

UNIVERSITY PRESS OF NEW ENGLAND publishes books under its own imprint and is the publisher for Brandeis University Press, Dartmouth College, Middlebury College Press, University of New Hampshire, University of Rhode Island, Tufts University, University of Vermont, Wesleyan University Press, and Salzburg Seminar.

ABOUT THE AUTHOR

Joe Wenderoth grew up near Baltimore. He graduated with a B.A. in English/ Creative Writing from Loyola College in Baltimore, attended the graduate Creative Writing program at New York University, then transferred to and received an M.F.A. from Warren Wilson College. To pay for food, shelter, and music, he has done and continues to do what he has to do.

LIBRARY OF CONGRESS CATALOGING-IN-PUBLICATION DATA

Wenderoth, Joe.
   Disfortune : poems / by Joe Wenderoth.
      p.   cm. — (Wesleyan poetry)
   ISBN 0-8195-2222-8. — ISBN 0-8195-1226-5 (pbk.)
   I. Title.   II. Series.
PS3573.E515D57   1995
811'.54—dc20   94—47185
♾